CLOS
to the

ALICE TAYLOR

With Drawings by Brian Lalor

BRANDON

First published 1989
Brandon Book Publishers Ltd
Dingle, Co. Kerry, Ireland

Poems © Alice Taylor 1989
Drawings © Brian Lalor 1989

ISBN 0 86322 103 3

Cover design: Paula Nolan
Cover photograph: Tony O'Gorman/*Irish Farmers Journal*
Typeset by Koinonia, Manchester
Printed by Richard Clay Ltd, Bungay

To Gabriel, because he believed

CONTENTS

WORDS

Words
Are messengers of thought,
A brush
Which on the canvas paints
A picture
That reflects the mind.
I pen these words
To paint my thoughts
Upon the pages here within:
Gently absorb
The scenes you find:
You have crossed the threshold
Of my mind.

CLOSE TO THE EARTH

Come to a quiet place,
A place so quiet
That you can hear
The grass grow.
Lie on the soft grass,
Run your fingers
Through the softness
Of its petals,
And listen:
Listen to the earth.
The warm earth,
The life pulse
Of us all.
Rest your body
Against its warmth;
Feel its greatness,
The pulse and throb,
The foundation
Of the world.
Look up into the sky,
The all-embracing sky,
The canopy of heaven.
How small
We really are:
Specks in the greatness
But still a part of it all.
We grow from the earth
And find
Our own place.

EARTH WOMAN

She was as real
As the dark brown
Bank of tiered turf
With the promise
Of warmer days.
She was as solid
As a great oak,
Unbending with
The winds that blow.
She was as strong
As the hard rocks
That weather the
Crushing waves.
Her core had
The luxuriant glow
Of the black, rich,
Sensuous soil.

PENNY WOMAN

Her heart is made of pennies,
Her mind is lined with pounds,
She's a special offer housewife
On a cut price merry-go-round.

WALK THE FIELDS

When I go home
I walk the fields,
The quiet fields
Where the warm dew
Had squelched between
My childish toes.
To sit beneath
The cool oak and ash
That sheltered
My adolescent dreams.
These trees stand
With leafy arms
Outstretched
Like lovers',
Not in passion
But with gentle
Sighs of contentment.
I watch the cows
Graze peaceful
Beside the river
Curving its way
Through furzed inches
Into the woods beyond.

This is a holy place
Where men have worked
Close to God's earth
Under the quiet heavens.

FREE TO BE CHILDREN

Give our children
Time to be children,
To savour the wonder
That is theirs.
To blossom in the world
Of their simplicity,
Not darkened
By the shadows
That are ours.

Let them bask
In the warmth
Of their sunshine,
Cleanse in the
Softness of their tears,
Be kissed by the
Beauties of nature,
Let them free
In the kingdom
That is theirs.

Their beauty
Is the purity
Of heaven,
Not tainted
By the ugliness
Of man.
Oh! let's not destroy
Their simplicity.
We never can
Improve
On what they have.

GOODBYE HOUSE

Vacuum womb house,
Contracted into a new life.
An afterbirth remaining,
Whispers and shadows
Of another day.
Memory on its
Soft grey clouds
Wafting through the rooms,
Webbing here
The part of me
That belongs.
The living that was blended
Through these stones,
So I take with me
Past soul of this house,
And leave behind
Part of mine.

THE MIND'S EYE

I have seen
With my mind's eye
Things to be written
Before I die.
Within my head
A subconscious shelf
Of details indexed
By another self.
Always there,
A second mind,
Ever probing
The scenes behind.
Beneath the deep
And flowing tide,
An inner depth,
Another side.
Mosses trail
As waters flow,
Roots grow buried
Down below.

DREAMS ON THE WING

Dreams are the wings of life
Which take you over clouds,
But to dream you fly alone,
You drift away from the crowd.
As a bird of the air you soar
And reach to the heights of delight,
Then glide back down to the earth
Refreshed by the vision of light.
In the mind are folded wings
You can open and fly to the stars;
Dreams are a wondrous gift
Not trapped by human bars.

HEALING PLACE

The frosty, feathery grass
Crunched beneath my feet
As my warm valley
Caressed me in welcome;
Bejewelled with frost
The trees and grass
Sparkled in the morning sun
And across the river
The mothering mountains
Shrouded in a misty light
Stood ground. Not a sound
But the gurgling of the river
And, companions of the solitary,
My feathered friends
Echoing my thoughts
Pouring forth their ecstasy
In unrestrained delight.

Oh, to hold these thoughts
And this beloved place
So much part of me
Forever in my mind.

I let this balm of my growing
Soak into my inmost soul,
To be written
On the back pages
Of my mind,
To be re-read
In some distant hour
When my need may be great
And I can no longer
Come to this my healing place.

CANCER

He was a man
Who took life
By the throat
And demanded what was his.
Moderation was not his theme,
Rather excess in all things,
Even in the greatness
Of his heart.
You could forgive him
Many faults
Because of so great a heart.
He lived life
With the spontaneity
Of a rushing river
That could not be blocked.
My heart ached to see him
Tubed by nose and hand,
Strapped like a wild creature
In his hospital bed;
A frightened animal,
Unaccustomed to restraint,
Brought in to shelter
From winter cold,
Eyes dilated in terror.
A man of hilly places
Trapped in antiseptic crucifixion;
Slow death dragged on for months,
This mighty man withered.
The torrent
Declined to a trickle
And then was no more.

COME SIT AWHILE

How nice to sit
And think awhile
Of little things
To make you smile,
Of silly things
You did in fun
Long ago
When you were young.
To think of people
Who were kind
And left a ray
Of light behind,
People who were
Nice to know
When you were young
Long time ago.
So come and sit
With me awhile
And think of things
To make us smile.

BURIED FREE

When I die
Don't bury me
In a military style,
Well-kept cemetery
Where everybody
Lies in rows
Of well organised,
Parallel toes.
I'd rather be
On hilly ground
Where mother nature's
Abundance flowers;
Beneath a mark
Of natural stone,
As bleached and grey
As will be my bones.
I could lie
Beneath a tree,
Whose whispering hair
Would shelter me.
Maybe long grass
And weeds would grow,
Better this
Than a military row.

CHAINS

I saw a bird
Upon a tree,
I smiled at him
He sang to me
And said, "Will you come today,
Come with me and fly away
Across the silent ocean wide,
Over yawning mountainside?
You will see the things that be,
That thrill my heart
And make me free."
I said, "I have things to do
So I cannot fly with you."
He looked at me
In a sad way
And sang, "You cannot fly today.
Because you're busy doing things,
You will never fly on wings.
You cannot soar above the sound,
You belong on solid ground."

PLEASE CALL

I am old,
I live alone:
Please don't leave me
On my own.
I sit on a chair,
I lie in bed,
Voluntary services keep me fed.
This is where I would be:
Please, please, call on me.
The clock goes tick,
The clock goes tock,
Please turn the key
That's in the lock.
The time is long,
The time goes slow;
Long hours alone,
I'm feeling low.
Please come
And chat awhile,
The human touch
Will make me smile.

TURN DOWN THE SOUND

Background music was the start
Of this all-pervasive sound;
It started as a soother,
Now it vibrates through the ground.
In the solitude of the great outdoors
Hear the music of the waves,
But the harmony is shattered
By transistors' howling wails.
Silence is broken:
We can no longer hear
The whispering of our mind
For the thunder in our ear.

TINKER WOMAN

I am married to a tinker man
We travel the roads in a scarlet van,
Carpets and bric-a-brac packed behind,
Ours is a special, roving mind.
In the winter when it is cold
Then I worry of growing old,
But in the spring and summer time
I wouldn't change your life for mine.
People do not like us near
What is it they have to fear?
We are only people without a place:
Do not turn away your face.

BENEATH A TREE

I lie on the grass
Beneath a tree,
The sky peeps down
Through the leaves at me;
It's cool in here
On this warm day,
A pale green haven
In the sun's hot ray.
I see a nest
Away up there,
Twigs interlaced
With horses' hair,
Firm built for
Fledglings' wear,
In a branch's arm
Of nature's care.
Now a butterfly
Comes into view,
Its white wings
Edged a delicate blue;
Then a bee
From the hives nearby,
Buzzing hello
As it passes by.
Fluttering through
The branches above,
On its way to rest
Comes a soft grey dove.
Its eyes peer down
With a solemn stare
As if to ask
What I'm doing here;
Then deciding

To wait and see
Its cooing voice
Serenading me.
A summer's day
Beneath a tree.

PLEASE CRY

Don't stand dry-eyed
Around my grave:
Bathe me
In the love I gave.
Pour your tears
On the earth below
To soften the thud
As down I go.
The only funeral
I would fear:
Where ne'er a one
Would shed a tear.

BODY SHELL

I walked through headstones
Old and grey
Recording people
Of another day.
Buried bones
And rotting flesh,
Residue of
Relentless death.
I saw dying
And it was hell
As the soul convulsed
From its earthly shell.
The soul is created
When a seed is set
Which bursts into life
With blood and sweat.
This life grows strong
Then fades away
And the soul escapes
From its house of clay.

MONSTER SEA

Timeless and tireless,
Resounding and pounding,
You are a grey-
Headed monster
Whose watery teeth
Relentlessly carve
The black-faced
Impregnable rocks
Tiered by centuries.
Cliffs towering
And menacing
Are the victims
Of your savage,
Barbaric onslaught,
Dark yawning holes
Eaten by your
Ravenous continuity
Bespeak your ferocity
By their very being.
Their majestic formation
Records aeons
Of repetitive attack
And victory must
Surely be yours
Because you are
Timeless.
Man is nothing
In your presence:
When the sap of our humanity
Has soaked into earth
You will swirl away the very
Marrow of our bones.

THIRST PRISON

Cold black nights
You led him home,
Gentle hand beneath his elbow
Preserving his precarious balance,
Maintaining his self-respect.
Many nights
Made miserable
By his insatiable thirst
Perfected your skill,
You the victim
More than he.
His life coloured
By alcoholic agony and ecstasy;
Yours a humdrum monotony
Of continual drudgery,
Your marriage
A life sentence
Of hard labour,
With no reprieve
For good behaviour.

MATURITY

The year has turned its coat of youth
Maturing into mellow hues,
Its growing pains and burning heat
Cooling now to calming ways.

BIRTH JOY

On the first day
Of the new year
You were born
Perfect and beautiful,
Ahead of schedule
But complete.
The agony
Of labour pains
Climaxing
In the joy
Of perfection achieved,
A little girl
The crowning glory.
Tears unrestrained
Poured on your
Downy head,
You were baptised
In streams of joy.

WATCH IT

Looked in the mirror
And I was there,
Ugly and sour-faced
With greasy hair.
And I asked myself,
Where have you gone?
What thorny bush
Have you sat upon?
And I said to myself,
Get off your butt
And pull yourself out
Of your poor-me rut.

I'M BUSY

She withered
On her virgin stem
(They all came
To see her then).
She had asked
If she could stay
With one of them
Till close of day;
But not one
Would let her in,
There is still no room
In Bethlehem inn.
They had called
But gave no more,
She died behind
Her closed door.
Don't ask me
To care for you,
I have other things
To do:
In this land
Where much
Wants more
You can die
Behind your door.

LOOKING FORWARD

The joy of
Anticipation,
Awaiting dreams'
Realisation
Looking forward
Is the fun
Of happy things
Yet to come.

CLINGING

Do not cling
To me
As ivy
To a tree,
Draining my strength,
Growing nothing
Of your own:
Stand tall
And we will grow
As two strong trees
Sheltering each other,
Our roots intertwining.

INNER SANCTUM

Let me steal five minutes
To welcome in the dawn
To touch its dewy fingers
As they creep across the lawn
To watch beneath a misty tree
The sun roll back the night
Its beams transfusing darkness
With soft translucent light
To hear the birds awake
With delight to greet the day
Let their happiness infuse me
To meet my day their way
Let this tranquil scene give balance
To the busy day ahead
To create a tranquil pool
For withdrawal inside my head.

CITY HEAT

Oh! the pain of this city street
The crowd
The noise
And the burning heat.
Oh! the joy of a mossy stream
Cool grass
Tall trees
And no human being.

TOGETHERNESS

Forced apart
By busy days
We who belong
Together,
As the interlaced
Fingers
Of praying
Hands,
Join again
In quiet times
At peace
In our
Togetherness.

ODE TO THE BLEACH TREES

I had walked
Where you had stood,
And this is a
Meaner place
For your going.

You who had grown
To elegant supremacy,
Lending grandeur
To our village,
Let us salute you!

You have been
Because a man
Looked to the future,
And we inherited.
Let us likewise
Leave behind us
Roots in the soil
Of Innishannon,
So that our children
May take shelter
Beneath the leaves
Of our foresight.

THE WISEING YEARS

You were unburnished gold
That polished warm
With the living years;
I had loved you
With a young girl's
Delectable fancy
But the wiseing years
Revealed your inner depth.
You have wrapped me
In the warm blankets
Of your love,
Your comforting arms
Sheltering me from
Life's icy draughts,
Warming our togetherness,
Creating in our life
An inner glow.

THE WOMAN OF GLEANNANARRIGLE

Her family, friends and neighbours
Chatted in groups in the graveyard.
On her coffin I placed
A bunch of autumn flowers
Laced with leaves dripping dew,
They had been picked
In a field that morning;
She had lived through
Her autumn years
And belonged to fields
And open places.
The undertaker stood
Silently there,
Not in sombre black
But in his Sunday best;
A kindly faced man,
A neighbour, and a friend
Telling him who I was,
By the name that was mine
When I lived across the river
From their valley.
A smile creased his face,
"I knew your father well."
We both looked into her grave
Where her coffin nestled
In hydrangia blooms
From her own garden.
"A good woman she was," he said.
"Yes," I agreed, "She often sent
Me a turkey for Christmas."
"You too," he smiled,
"For twenty years I had

A Gleannanarrigle turkey
And a bag of spuds for Christmas."
A big woman with a big heart.
"Her daughter-in-law seems nice."
"Hand picked," he said. "She was hand picked."
He looked across the fields
At her old home.
"She left things in good hands,
She was sound to the very end."

I WAS HAPPY THEN

 A sunny morning,
Running barefoot
Through dew-drenched grass
Picking buttercups:
I was happy then.

Wedding evening,
Together on a train
Thundering into the future,
Alone at last:
I was happy then.

A delivery ward,
Muzzy with exhaustion;
Holding a little girl,
Perfection achieved:
I was happy then.

Holding in my hand
My very own book;
My thoughts realized,
Dreams in substance:
I was happy then.

Hanging on a wall
My painting in oils;
Easy on the eye,
A wish realized:
I was happy then

So many nights
Of close enchantment
With one so dear,

To be so loved:
I was happy then.

I remember
The good times,
The rough ones too.
They were my life:
I am happy now.

A TOUCH OF SPRING

Spring came today
And walked with me
Up the hill,
Breathing softness in the air,
Opening gates within my head.
The birds felt his presence,
Pouring forth symphonies
Of unrestrained welcome.
It was mid-January
And he just came
To have a peep,
Trailing behind him
Along the valley
Wisps of purple veils.

FRESH FLOWERS

Give me a bunch
Of dew-fresh flowers,
What if they will not last:
I cannot live in the future
The present is all I ask.

HELLO

Your soft voice was sad
On the phone just now.
Not a grave word was said
But your melancholy
Seeped along the wires
And into my listening ear.
You were gone into
Your own inner world,
Floating passively around
In your piscean waters.
Today you could paint
And your picture would be
Soft and misty, with a
Blue haze, where you could
Lose the reality of life.

TWO ENDS

Sunday mass,
Two wheelchairs
By the rails:
An old lady,
Quiet, inert
Sleeping place
Waiting for
The final rest;
A little child
Vital and alive
Trapped on two
Useless legs,
Travesty of
Childhood.

God, what was
In Your mind?

YOUNG PAIN

When I was young
I crashed into stone walls
And broke my heart.
"Easy," adults cautioned, "easy,"
But I flew to the peaks of joy and
Dazzled by the sun hit unseen rocks,
Crashing into pools of black despair.
Flailing around in adolescent waters
I ecstasied and agonised,
Finally floating into calmer ways
Where life became more bearable,
But never again as beautiful.

A RUSTY LOVE AFFAIR

In a sun-baked shed
With black-grained hands
These iron men of steam
Sweat oil pursuing an ideal.
There she sits in state,
This queen of the past,
Waiting for her archaic
Limbs to be greased
Into motion, her joints
Soothed gently by her
Black lovers, unquestioning
In their complete adoration.
In this brown station yard
Carriages grey with old age,
Retired queens proudly wear
The grandeur of another day.
Here, a dream in creation,
An old train being reborn
When men become gods
Breathing life into dead iron.

UP AT THE CASTLE

Like a butterfly
You wafted into
The old stone coach house,
Telling gently of fifty years
Service up at the castle.
Your calm eyes were
Dark brown pools
Of laughing secrets,
And yet your face
Had the open innocence
Of a child untouched by life;
You spoke of "the family"
And great kindness shown.
They must have sheltered you
And yet those eyes had
Savoured secret ecstasies;
You had tasted their nectar
But like an elusive butterfly
Had escaped their nets.

THE MEN WITH SCYTHES

When the graveyard became overgrown
And headstones were buried in grass
Then they came,
The men with scythes,
Weather-beaten farming men
Who worked steadily
At their own pace,
Edged and cut
With the calm determination
Of those who endlessly
Work the fields.
The crack of blade on stone
Brought forth blessings
On the dead;
Uncovering the resting place
Of an old friend
Stirred forgotten memories
Recalled with wit and fun.
As the moon rose
Behind the steeple
Order was restored
And headstones stood
Proud and free,
The living giving
Dignity to the dead.

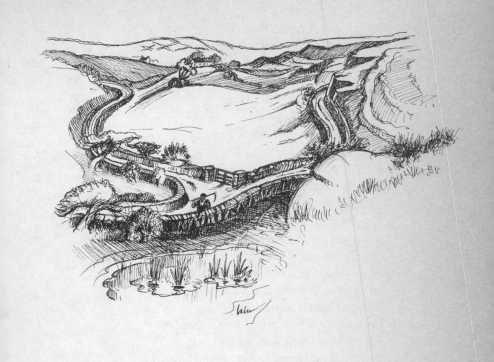

A SCHOOL FRIEND

We walked to school
Through the dew-drenched fields
Meeting where our paths crossed
At the foot of a grassy hill.
If one ran late, the other
Left a stone message
On the mossy bridge.
He had muddy boots,
A jumper torn by briars
And hair that went its own way.
Trivial details to a mind
That raced amongst the clouds
And followed rabbits down brown burrows.
Gentle hands, twisted by a bad burning,
Reached out towards the birds,
And they perched on his fingers
At ease with one of their own.
Blessed with a mind that ran free
From the frailties of his body
He walked during his quiet life
Close to the gates of heaven.

THE HOMECOMING

The king was dead
And the birds flew home,
But there was no tree to perch on.
He had been quiet and private
And his queen who had filled his nest
With gaiety and colour
Had died twenty years before;
The fledglings had scattered
And the shattered king
Was picked up by a swooping hawk
Who ravaged his life
Chasing the young ones away.
Finally, with broken wings,
He crept back to his own
And gently closed his eyes.
They brought him home
Past the old nest
And laid him beside his queen,
They were together again
At peace for ever.

SEARCHING

What do you seek?
Is it the virgin spring
Buried beneath the rock,
Or do you dream back
For water under the bridge?

What do you seek?
Is it the unattainable bubble
Just beyond your fingertips,
Or the dark, deep earth
Beneath your feet?

What do you seek?
Is it the memory
Of summers past,
Or the beckoning finger
Of the misty future?

What do you seek?

JUST AS YOU ALWAYS WERE

You tore the roots of childhood
From deep inside my heart
And left a gaping wound
Dripping with memory tears.
You had walked beside me
Along the ploughed furrow,
Sometimes ahead if sods were rough,
Then behind if my need was open field;
Now no longer here
But gone to sunlit pastures.
Help me not to stumble
But to rejoice in your happy state
Because yours was a smiling God.
Your time will have been in vain
If I do not carry on
As you had done so many times,
And I will think of you
And meet you in my mind
Because barriers are man made
And you are with our God,
Waiting, loving and caring me,
And I will reach out to you
When my need is great
And you will be there
Just as you always were.

BATTERED CHALICE

God's day,
The birds and sun
Celebrate his creation.
You pick the daisies
With such joy in your hands;
Little child in the body of a man,
You are the host
In a battered chalice.
"Daoine le Dia," old people said,
And how wise they were
Because you live within
The circle of God's arm;
Not for you
The snares of this world,
You walk above man's narrow vision.

COBWEB OF OLD AGE

Dear gentle soul
Do not think
You are a burden:
In your love
You conceived them
And wove them
Into the fabric
Of your life,
Giving to them
All your strength.
The tide has turned,
They are the strong,
And you have your
Delicate threads
Caught in the cobweb
That is old age.
They would wrap
You in their strength,
Let them now
Because you can
Give them much
Of gentleness
And the wisdom
Of your time.

A SHARED LIGHT

She was in the book queue,
A pretty girl with eyes
Full of black pain.
"I had a miscarriage,"
She said. "A first baby
After many waiting years.
It tore me apart and
I found great comfort
In your book.
It healed my heart
And gave me hope."

I think of her now,
Grateful because
We gave each other
Light.

SPECIAL CHILD

With soft hands you caressed my hair
And touched my face with child kisses,
Looking into your eyes of love
I saw inside
The tabernacle of the Lord.
Special child, you are so loved
That no earthly doubts
Have touched your saintly essence,
Leaving heaven's gate ajar
You live within a beam
Untouched by man.
May the world move gently with you
As you walk above its roughness.

WITHOUT FOUNDATION

He swayed
On the dance floor,
An overgrown weed
Fertilized by alcohol.
He surveyed
The swirling throng
With a practised eye,
Selecting the possibilities
With most to offer.

Later, swaying now
To the beat of the drum,
Wearing around his neck
A female trophy,
Heads buried in necks,
Occasionally
Coming up for air
To exchange
Slobbering inebriated kisses.

In later years
Marriage counsellors
Pondered
Problems of communication.

BACK TO SIMPLICITY

Oh, clergyman all dressed in black,
What a mighty church is at your back.
We are taught that by your hand
We must be led to our promised land.
Jesus is locked in your institutions
Of ancient laws and resolutions,
Buried so deep and out of sight
That sometimes we cannot see the light,
Behind huge walls that cost so much
Where simple things are out of touch.
But could it be He is not within
These walls so thick, with love so thin?
Does he walk on distant hills
Where long ago He cured all ills?
Is He gone out to open places
To simple people, all creeds, all races?
Is Jesus gone from off the altar
Catching fish down by the water?
Is He with the birds and trees,
Gathering honey with the bees?
Could it be in this simple way
That God meant man to kneel and pray?

LAST FAREWELL

She stood at my bedside,
A momentary presence;
Soft smiling face
Of earlier years.
For weeks she had wasted
With an incurable illness;
Now she raised her hand
In a last, sad farewell
And was gone from beside me.
Tomorrow I knew they would come
And tell me she was dead.

GOLDEN FLOWER

Tender, beautiful love,
A golden sunflower
Deep-rooted in the earth
Within my heart,
Kissed by the warm rays
Of he who gave it life.
I lay no claim or right
To this golden flower;
It is a bonus to my life
Growing in the walled garden
Of my heart.
And when winter falls
Within my mind
I withdraw to this sunny place
And warm my frozen thoughts
In the embracing radiance
Of this golden flower.

COMMUNION

Warm bodies
Close together
Kindling feelings
Deep within,
Fanned by memories
Of former ectasies.

Close friends
And lovers,
Mind, heart
And body
Joined in harmony,
Complete communion
Of human kind.

FIRST PARTING

It hurts me so
To see him thus
My babe
Of tender years,
Clutching
At his little sack,
Choking back
His tears.
I long to shelter
In my arms
This little lad
Turned four,
But I will
Take him by the hand
And lead
Him out the door.
Into a world
Where he must have
The courage
To stand alone,
Strengthened
By the love
That he has known
At home.
And I must learn
To let him go
Though helping
When I can,
My little son
Now taking
His first steps
To being
A man.

SEPARATION

In their own corner
As two saplings
They grew together,
Their branches intertwining,
Creating a life tree:
Thorns of winter
Leaves of spring
Warmth of summer
Blending them into one
During a lifetime of growth.

Then one cold December night
A great storm raged,
Tearing their branches apart,
Breaking their togetherness
Till she lay still in the earth
And he stood bent
With his limbs broken,
The freezing winter winds
Howling around
His unprotected roots.

A WALK

To go to the fields
When the work is done
And a mantle of ease
O'er the day has come;
To sit on a stone,
Watch the Bandon flow,
And the white moon rise
O'er old Knockroe.

A MEMORY

The waste ground was choked with weeds
That grew above her head
But in the middle of this waste
One flower of golden red.

The little child came every day
To gaze upon this scene
The flower it was the loveliest sight
That she had ever seen.

This flower took root and blossomed
It grew inside her head
And led her on to lovely things
Long after it was dead.

ROOTS

I have grown here
For many years,
Warm and safe
In my own place.
A lifetime of being here
Makes me feel secure;
My roots grow deep
Into the warm earth.
Now I am old
My branches are tattered,
But still I would stay here
Because this is where I belong.
Do not dig me up:
The damage to my branches
Will ease me slowly from this place,
But pull up my roots
And my whole being will break.

UNFORGIVEN

Dear God if I do wrong
And am forgiven,
Please give me the grace
To forgive myself
Lest this wrongdoing
Becomes a cancer
In my soul
And I become
A self-righteous person
To camouflage my
Unforgiven sin.

A HAPPY DAY

Across the golden amber sand
I watched the sunlit sea,
The waves were sparkling in the sun
And laughing back at me.
Out they danced and in they raced
And tumbled in the caves,
I think that I shall never see
Such happy things as waves.

A GREAT TREE

You stand there
In splendid isolation,
A remote stillness
Centred in a green field,
Your praying arms
Held forth
In majestic supplication.
Shrouded in your
Green leafy veils
Of mysterious depths,
What a tranquil, untouchable
World of nature
You portray.

A PLOUGHED FIELD

Oh brown ploughed field
What an ancient skill
Is in your turned sod.
A skill inherited
By generations of earthy men.
Beneath the sheltering trees
You cover the hillside
In a cloak of brown velvet.
What a softness is yours;
You are an open book
Yet to be written;
The virginity of the upturned sod
Waiting to be fertilised
By the hands of man
And nurtured by the warmth of nature.

A NEIGHBOURHOOD

Be kind
When you talk
Of me
With your friends.
My public image
Is a light
Shining
From my rooftop:
Do not shatter it
With a steel-pointed arrow.
Fragmented glass
Breaks
Other images,
So let all lights
Shine
And make this
A warm place
For living.

BEREAVEMENT

Your suffering was terrible to see.
I suffered for you
But I was in an outer circle,
No one could reach inside
The torture chamber of your mind.
Your gaping wounds could not be touched
They had to be licked clean by you,
Like a wounded animal in its lair
You lay bleeding for many months.
The numbness gone
You crawled forward
Into a darker tunnel,
But this at least led out
From your lonely lair.
Now you prayed
And cried to heaven for mercy,
I held your hand
But I could not lead you
From this place.
An inner strength
Born of a greater power
Could only bring you through.
And then it came to help you
And so you stumbled on
Gaining strength from a source
Greater than your sorrow.
And on the day you smiled
Your first real smile,
I thanked God
That with his help
Any burden could be borne.

DEFEATED

I am weary
And a cold apathy
Oozing through my bones
Makes movement meaningless;
A dead weight
Crushing my mind
Blocks my forward path
And fills my mind with grey.
I could stay here,
Motionless for ever
In a nook of forgetfulness,
Letting the mainstream course on;
And when the final flood
Would swirl the river down
I would be carried on its crest
Into the final waters beyond.

KINDNESS

The warmth of your kindness
Kept me in my mind;
Its worth could not be measured,
It had goodness undefined;
You held out a caring hand
When I was full of pain;
You thawed my frozen being
And made me live again.

THE HONEY TREE

The day was soft and mellow,
Growth was in the ground;
I went into the garden,
Climbed to the honey sound,
Eased my spade through the fallen leaves
Of golden brown and red
And as I lifted out the earth
I made a soft brown bed.
Mother nature opened wide
Her arms of velvet brown
And on her maternal lap
I sat my young tree down.
All around the soft young roots
I folded mother earth
And when my baby tree stood tall
I felt joy as in a birth.
I lashed her to a firm stake
To hold her in the sways,
A seasoned piece of older wood
To guard her growing days.

PLEASE DON'T

Don't put money in my Christmas stocking
Don't take away my fun,
I believe in magic moments
Don't put clouds across my sun.
My life is full of golden wonders
Heaven's rays still beam on me,
Let me weave my golden dreams
Let me my joy of make-believe.
Fairies dance on silver dew drops
Tossing gold dust through my days,
My golden days are so happy
Don't dark them with your adult ways.

JANUARY

We do not like you January
You are cold, hard and wet,
Gripping the countryside
In a frozen death.
Christmas cheer is darkened,
Virgin snow to slush,
Howling icy winds
Replace the holy hush.
Dark and reptile roads
With black ice out of sight,
Trap the cheery driver
And kill him in the night.
January you're the Judas
Of the twelve around the year,
You make the lonely lonelier
And the old to fear.

WINTER BLIZZARD

Dear Lord
Does a cold anger
Fill your heart
Is it coming
Down in snow
As a blizzard
On the land
Are you weeping
Tears of ice
Have we frozen
All your love
Are the icicles
Of heaven
A judgement
From above?

ALL WET DAYS

All her days were wet ones
And all her thoughts were sad
And anytime you met her
You would regret you had.
She'd depress you drip by drip
And leave you feeling low:
She is a wet day woman
And will be always so.

NOBODY TOLD THE COWS

The cattle seek
The sheltering hedge,
Instinct leading them
Away from cold winds;
But the hedge is gone
And now they stand by
The electric fence,
Cold rains slashing
Against exposed rumps.

UNFORGIVEN THIEF

She spoke to me
From ravaged mid-life eyes,
"I was sexually abused at six
It went on for a long time
Where was my mother then?
The bastard stole my childhood
Sullied everything clean in me
Savaged my unborn sexuality
May he rot in hell for ever.
The joy of forgiveness
Can never flower for me:
He brutally destroyed
The innocence of my soul.
An eternity of misery
Is not too great a payment
For a burnt out childhood
And a lifetime of scorched memories."

THEN

An early spring morning
Nobody on the beach but us.
We came searching
For oiled birds
And found only
Sparkling sunbeams
Riding bareback
On leaping waves,
A sunlit world
Alive with sea music.
It was a picture
To be painted
When the scene was fresh;
I cannot
Now recall
All the magic
That was then.

WINTER TREES
(OUTSIDE MY WINDOW)

The window is wet
With running tears,
And swirling rain
Blows in grey curtains
Over the dark trees
Which shelter under their
Leafbare winter coats
In the wood across,
While the black river
Bathes their cold toes
Under a laden, metallic
January sky.

A READING WINDOW

Moonlight phantoms
Frosty pictures
On a latticed
Window pane.
A smiling dolphin
King in a peasant's hat
Rebel behind steel glass
Craggy hill in sea
Knower unknown,
Softly illuminated
By a milky
Street lamp
In a Dingle
Dawn window.

FREE WHEELING

Come night
You cannot jump into bed
And make love with her
If you kicked football
In her mind all day.
Her days
Are an overflow
Of harmony
From her nights;
So her love
Is a cycle
Of day and night
That keeps her life
Running free.

COMPLETE

Making love
You span mountains
Walk on treetops
And swim in the sea mist
Of your mind.

Making love
A fusion of
Inner and outer being
In an explosion of tranquility
That is complete.

MAN OF DINGLE

Black lumps of coal
Eyes quarried in
A Kerry mountain
Face of brown heather
Edged about by
A knotty hilly bush
Curled against the sea
On a windswept
Dingle coast.
Quietly observing
Frothy people and waves
Washing around
Your imperturbable
Rocklike presence,
Listening to sounds,
Absorbing, sifting,
Ruminating and
Occasionally
Dropping forth
Single words
Laden with the
Salty essence
Of the deep
Outer harbour.

RUBBISH

The dustbins stood outside the school
Waiting for the refuse truck,
A high-class mongrel chancing by
Nosed in to try his luck.

With years of past experience
He tossed aside the cover,
And foraged in its smelly depths
To see what he'd discover.

He tossed trash on the footpath
As only mongrels will,
And with a watery blessing
He sauntered up the hill.

The dustmen came and took the bins
Left the rubbish on the ground,
They are not paid to gather it
Just to lift bins on the round.

Parents, teachers, children
Walked round it every day,
Education was their quest
So they passed it on their way.

So who picks up the rubbish
The mongrels scatter round?
The answer to that question
Is walked into the ground.

POOR ME!

I know I must not
Get up-tight;
I must relax
And see things right.
People put my nerves
On edge,
Between my eyes
They drive a wedge.
A heavy load
Is on my back,
A pony carrying
A horse's pack.
Tension a knot
Within my head,
Tightened by something
Somebody said.
I snapped at a remark
I should have let pass.
Could it be I'm becoming
A pain in the arse?

AND SO TO SLEEP

After he had died
I sat beside his bed.
A soothing peace
Filled the room
And the trees
Outside the window
Sighed in contentment.
Minutes before
He was there,
Then closing his eyes
As effortlessly
As the autumn leaves
He wafted
To his golden harvest.
His last weeks
Easing out his roots,
Nestled in the bosom
Of his family
Till his final benediction
To die at home
In his own bed
His circle of life
Complete.

JACKEY'S GARDEN

Here there is no set layout,
Nature's freedom is all about.
A garden cared by loving hands,
Green profusion with nothing planned.

Flowers and shrubs freely abound.
Bees in their hive hum a mellow sound.
No regimented hedge in orderly array,
This is a garden with nature's sway.

A haven created by a man of love,
Man of the earth, with thoughts of above.
Here nature, love and care combine
To create a refuge, an escape from time.

JIM

Just across the road
Jim lived in a shed;
It wasn't very big,
Just enough to hold his bed.
He was never lonely,
He chatted on the street,
A kindly neighbour fed him
So he had enough to eat.
But it didn't seem right
Him sleeping in the cold;
Something should be done
As Jim was getting old.
So he went into a home
Where everything was right,
And everyone felt good
Now Jim was in by night.
But when I went to see him
His face a story told;
His body was dry and warm
But his eyes were lost and cold.
Jim had lived here too long
To dig up his ancient roots;
His body now had comfort
But his heart was in his boots.
Jim died then in September,
Died in a spotless bed,
But he had died six months before,
The day he left the shed.

MAISIE

She is so very frail,
Her legs are pencil thin,
The blue veins a craggy ridge
Beneath her parchment skin.
In the village she's the oldest
With a mind designed to last,
Her memory is so clear
She can reach into the past.
Her heart is bright and easy
Her thoughts are light and gay,
Though in years she is December
Her heart stayed young as May.

SHIPPOOL WOOD

Shippool wood tranquil and deep:
How peaceful to dream
With your trees asleep.
Wrapped in your leafy arms so quiet,
Shielded from all but dappled daylight.

Nothing here but peace alone,
Birds and rabbits, nature's own.
Under the wing of the elm and oak
To sit and let the silence soak
In through your body, into your mind:
This is a sanctuary for human kind.

MORNING SHADOWS

My home in the morning
Is fusing with light,
The shadows are wearing
The coat tails of night.
The softness of dawn
Is wrapping us round,
Softly eroding
Skulking night hound.

RETURN TO INNISHANNON

When I am drained within
And the light
Which leads me on
Is quenched
I come to this place
To be healed:
Its twin spires
Reach out to me
In a warm embrace
And I know
That I have come back
To my own place.

I have lived my life
Far from here
But I have taken
This little place
In the walled garden
Of my heart
To rekindle
My tranquility.
And when my lifespring
Begins to fade
I make a pilgrimage
Back to my own place.